I AM MY BROTHER'S KEEPER

Empowering Men To Take Their Place

Ps. 8:4-6

Bishop Van I. Sharpe

BISHOP VAN I. SHARPE

I AM MY BROTHER'S KEEPER

Empowering Men To Take Their Place

PENDIUM
PUBLISHING HOUSE
514-201 DANIELS STREET
RALEIGH, NC 27605

For information, please visit our Web site at
www.pendiumpublishing.com

PENDIUM Publishing and its logo
are registered trademarks.

I AM MY BROTHER'S KEEPER
VAN I. SHARPE

ISBN: 978-1-936513-92-5

PUBLISHER'S NOTE

Unless otherwise indicated, Bible quotations are taken from The Authorized
King James Version, Copyright 2000 by The Zondervan Corporation,
and The Amplified Bible, Copyright 1954, 1958, 1964, 1965, 1987 by
The Lockman Foundation, and The Message: The Bible in Contemporary
Language, Copyright 2002 by Eugene H. Peterson, and The Living Bible,
Copyright 1971 by Tyndale House Publishers, Wheaton, Illinois, and The
New International Version of the Bible, Copyright 1973, 1978, 1984 by
International Bible Society.

Front cover photograph of the author by Terry Johnson
P.O. Box 1411, Tarboro, NC 27886
Tel. 252-469-5188   Email: tireman7212@gmail.com

This book is printed on acid-free paper.

This book is dedicated to every man striving to be impactful and serve your family and your generation.

ABOUT THE AUTHOR

Bishop Van I. Sharpe is a resident and native of Tarboro, N.C. He is a graduate from Tarboro High School in Tarboro and graduated Magna Cum Laude with a B. A. degree in Mass Communications from Shaw University in Raleigh, N.C. He is the pastor and founder of Newness of Life Christian Center in Tarboro N.C. He is married to Resunester Sharpe, and they are the proud parents of one lovely daughter, Vanneika Aireesh Sharpe, one handsome grandson, Taiden Rashad, and one beautiful granddaughter, Adaylyn. His ministry includes pastoring, developing and overseeing leaders, flowing in the prophetic, and evangelizing in various states.

Bishop Van Sharpe
Newness Of Life Christian Center
P.O. Box 1462 / 936 Albemarle Avenue
Tarboro, NC 27886
252-641-0098
E-mail: *godisable@embarqmail.com*
Web Address: *www.newnessoflifechristiancenter.org*

Contents

ACKNOWLEDGEMENTS

Glory and Honor be unto God for his good hand being upon me as I wrote every word of this book. I know your Son, Jesus and the Holy Spirit are the keys to helping all men be great!

Special thanks to my beautiful wife, Resunester Sharpe whose love and support help me to move forward.

Thank you Beverly Reynolds for your superb editing skills! You are such a delight to work with. Also I want to give a special shout out to my brother-in-law, Frankie Reynolds.

Special thanks to my immediate family, my darling mother, Shirley Sharpe, my sisters, (Pastor Susan Sharpe and Gloria Boyd), my brother Bishop Wayne (his wife, Pastor Marjorie), my daughter, Vanneika, my grandson, Taiden Sharpe, and my granddaughter Adaylyn Sharpe.

Thank you Newness of Life for allowing me the time to give myself to this book as I strive to lead you into your inheritance. You're the best!

INTRODUCTION

MEN OFF PAUSE

Zig Ziglar said, "You can succeed at almost anything for which you have unbridled enthusiasm." Therefore, I know that writing this book is part of my assignment in the earth because I have unbridled enthusiasm to see men get their lives off pause and moving in the direction of their destiny. I am enthusiastic about causing men to understand that other men are pleading and in desperate need of their help and encouragement. Some refuse to admit it, yet many are beginning to admit it and reach out to other men for motivation and confirmation.

Men are breaking away from their adversary, the devil and his lie that their lives have to remain on pause, going nowhere, forward or backward. When you hit the pause button on your DVD player, you see the picture on the screen, but it is not moving. The person or persons aren't going anywhere. There is a lack of action or activity. That's how Satan wants men today: on the scene but doing nothing to move the family or community forward. He wants us on Pause, in the local jail or in prison. Satan wants us doing nothing to help pay the bills, doing nothing to help send the kids to college, doing nothing to lift the church or the pastor's hand in the kingdom. However, many men through the help of our concerned brothers in Christ are calling the devil a liar.

Men are beginning to understand that declining levels of testosterone in the natural doesn't mean a declining life in the spiritual if they have other great men around them that will function as keepers. Those who do will help you get your kick in life back!

As you read this book, I pray that you will get the help you need in order to become the help your brother needs. He needs it a lot more than he is willing to admit because he is afraid you will kill him instead of aiding him in his manhood. He needs a brother like you that will reassure him that his time has come to face this culture head on and overcome it. He needs you to help him face depression, anger, fatigue, anxiety, memory loss, relationship problems, loss of sex drive, erectile dysfunction etc. He needs you as he deals with drugs and crime in his community. He needs you as he deals with being laid off from his job or problems in ministry. He not only needs the support of his wife (female), but he needs the support of male brothers.

As you read this book it is my hope that you become better as a man and more effective in being your brother's keeper. I know we haven't mastered this, but we must never ever stop trying to get better at it everyday. Let's hit the play button and get this party started!

YOU ARE NOT HER CHILD

It is necessary I believe to write a section in this book that informs every man to reclaim his manhood. We have been raised by our mothers and fathers. In some cases many men have only been raised by a mother's love and influence. Having a mother telling you what to do was ok for a particular season of your life. She nursed you and took care of you when you were a child, but many women fail to release their boys to a male's influence. She continues to want to tell this grown man what to do and where to go. This causes rebellion in the man and resentment towards his mother and future wife. Every woman in his mind will seem to be nagging and annoying. He automatically can't stand being married to a woman who is trying to tell him what to do and he resents or pushes aside the information given to him by her even if she is right.

Many women fail to follow the example of Hannah who released her son to a man. Hannah leaves her son, Samuel with Eli. The word **Eli** means "lofty or ascension." It means "to mount up." We should always seek to let our sons be raised or in the presence of a man that is moving upward. He should be one who is going up spiritually and naturally.

I was talking to one of my brothers in Christ recently who is a multi-millionaire. One of the things that we discussed was "Mindset." The main thing he stated that caused his life to shift and move to another level was when he asked a millionaire pastor that he served in ministry to let him see how the millionaire lived. He stated when he saw how God had blessed the man of God and the opportunities and possibilities that were available to him if he served and obeyed God, his thinking shifted to a new dimension. God began to put business ideas in his spirit and today he has several thriving businesses. I call him an Apostle of Finance because his desire is to be a blessing to leaders and ministries and I believe he will eventually help raise up other millionaires in the body of Christ. I believe it will happen by the grace of God.

Hannah put Samuel in a place where he could be groomed for his kingdom assignment. Women often don't give their sons a chance to be in the presence of successful men. Their sons can't continue to be exposed to thugs and hoodlums and reach their destiny. The sooner they can be around the house of God and godly men the better. Notice these verses,

> 1 Samuel 1:22-28 *"But Hannah went not up; for she said unto her husband, I will not go up until the child be weaned, and then I will bring him, that he may appear before the Lord, and there abide for ever. [23] And Elkanah her husband said unto her, Do what seemeth thee good; tarry until thou have weaned him; only the Lord establish his word. So the woman abode, and gave her son suck until she weaned*

him. [24] And when she had weaned him, she took him up with her, with three bullocks, and one ephah of flour, and a bottle of wine, and brought him unto the house of the Lord in Shiloh: and the child was young. [25] And they slew a bullock, and brought the child to Eli. [26] And she said, Oh my lord, as thy soul liveth, my lord, I am the woman that stood by thee here, praying unto the Lord. [27] For this child I prayed; and the Lord hath given me my petition which I asked of him: [28] Therefore also I have lent him to the Lord; as long as he liveth he shall be lent to the Lord. And he worshipped the Lord there."

As a man you are chosen to lead, not be a child. Men who are walking in their manhood relate to you in such a way that will cause your development to take place speedily. A lot of mother's treat their grown sons as baby boys. The boys become men who are unprepared to lead their home as well as lead successfully in the house of God. They only want to be pampered or marry women who do all the work. Many women start out thinking that it's okay to marry a man like this, but eventually it becomes too big a cross for them to bear. They become overwhelmed trying to raise the children plus this man who is still trying to be a baby. He might not be a bad person, but he has been groomed incorrectly for the task that he is now a partaker of.

I believe every man should desire that his wife or fiancée talk to him like a man or as a husband instead of a child. This requires that she reverences him. If this isn't done, it cripples us as men and causes us to feel small. Many men even become so angered by it that they walk out or away from the conversation while the wife is talking. Some men let the wife keep talking but really don't listen to anything she says. They shut her out. Others become so agitated by the way they are being talked to that they tell their wives or fiancée to shut up. Still there are other men who become so enraged that they hit or beat the female. All of these ways are the wrong way to handle the situation. We as men need to know that God's word addresses this issue.

> Ephesians 5:33 *"Nevertheless let every one of you in particular so love his wife even as himself; and the wife see that she reverence her husband."*

This powerful verse tells us that our wives are to respect us. Yet, if they don't, we can't lash out at them or hit them. We have to trust God to deal with her about her responsibility to reverence us. God can cause her to repent and see the error of her ways. Our responsibility is to continue to behave as men. Most women have not been groomed to respect men. Even though a woman should respect her husband or fiancée, many refuse to do it or don't know how to do it. Satan uses this to cause a man to feel castrated.

You can't pout or hit the woman that you love. Violence toward her is never the right thing to do. She is your helper. Let her gently know that her respect is very important to you because even if you get it from everyone else and not from her, it doesn't mean as much. Tell her in a loving way that you are there to provide and protect her. Remember, "You are not her child."

HOW TO DEAL WITH AN OVERBEARING WOMAN

Recently in our country a famous lady was asked how she was able to maintain a good marriage relationship for over seventeen years when she answered that the major key for her was "Submission," many people became upset. She had to explain to them that she married a man that could lead her and that she had great respect for her husband. She also stated to them that she wasn't being treated like a doormat or made to feel small, but she didn't see the word submission as a bad word.

Thank God for this woman who understands the order of God. She understands that submission doesn't have to hurt her. She looks at it the same way the church is submissive to Christ. Our Lord doesn't hurt or mistreat us. Submission isn't seen by the true church as a bad move, but it is the only righteous move for us to make, especially if we want to function effectively as the church and make a significant impact in the earth. This woman and other women who allow their husbands to lead them know how to build their houses instead of tearing them down.

> Proverbs 14:1 *"Every wise woman buildeth her house: but the foolish plucketh it down with her hands."*

Because you and I are living in a world that is marching out of step with God, we have a lot of mind renewal for men to do as leaders. When most women who are independent come into the relationship, they come in strong willed and ready to continue to run things. Many men in order to keep her from fussing or to keep her happy give in to her. This causes the overbearingness to increase. As the relationship continues, he relinquishes more and more and the spirit of the woman intensifies, and she now orders him around.

Talk show hosts and other men constantly say, "You can't have any peace in your house unless you make your wife happy." So we have men constantly made to submit and let women rule. This causes most people to believe the words and song of Beyoncé "Who run the world? Girls." Instead, they might quote the words of James Brown, "It's a man's world, but it wouldn't be nothing, nothing without a woman or a girl."

According to the Bible James Brown was closer to stating the truth. I am not dealing with the rest of the words in the songs because I don't know them nor desire to know the songs. I am only dealing with the main chorus of them both. Let's examine the scriptures,

> 1 Corinthians 11:8-9 *"For the man is not of the woman; but the woman of the man. [9] Neither was the man created for the woman; but the woman for the man."*

1 Timothy 2:13-14 *"For Adam was first formed, then Eve. [14] And Adam was not deceived, but the woman being deceived was in the transgression."*

These scriptures aren't to be used to beat women down nor to push men up. They were written so that we could understand God's order. They were written so we could function and operate in our role properly. It is important that women aren't overbearing. This causes her to be out of place and lose her beauty in the sight of God. She also loses her beauty in the eyes of every true man who knows and understands order. Also, every man who allows himself to be told what to do and refuses to lead loses his masculinity and looks like a wimp to God and in the eyes of every true woman who knows and understands her place. She really doesn't want to lead. She wants you to lead or get out in front.

The word overbearing means domineering, dictatorial, haughtily or rudely arrogant. It means to bear over or down by weight or force. I became a believer at age nineteen so most of my adult life has been in the kingdom of God. I have seen some women give their husband a look and scare them half to death. I've seen women so domineering that they make a motion towards their husband and their husbands leave the church without finishing their kingdom duties. These haughty women if not given control aren't happy in the house of God and usually they seek to go where their man is made to feel powerless while she feels empowered. She acts and functions as a rude, arrogant woman.

Far too many Christian and non-Christian men are letting their wives call the shots. It is repulsive to even hear men talk as if their opinion means nothing at all. There is only one way to deal with an overbearing woman, "Stand up." It won't seem like it will work at first because this overbearing woman that has been out of her place for years will resist the idea of giving up headship. Even though she is out of order a bad habit has been created, and you and I both know bad habits aren't easily broken. You, as the head of the house, must continue to Stand Up. Again let me remind you that I am not talking about being hateful or being disrespectful towards your spouse. Cursing at your spouse is not the answer. But you must Stand up in love. Deep down inside if she is a true woman of God who sincerely cares about you and the family she will honor and love you for it later. She will know she has a true leader in the house. She will know she has a man that seeks to honor her.

I recognize some men are dealing with women who have been physically and verbally abused. You will have to explain to your spouse that you aren't seeking to be abusive or put her down in any way, but you want to lead her. Explain to her in love that you and she together can achieve your goals as she respects your role as head. Think about as you read this book when the President walks in a room, and we are asked to stand; we do it. When the judge walks into the courtroom, we stand as well. We don't stand because we are afraid of them (male or female). We do it because we respect the position that they are in and the position deserves our respect. We must know that husband (man) is a position. It is a higher position than wife (woman). The final decision is the man's. But he must always take into consideration his wife's desire or request.

> 1 Peter 3:1 *"Likewise, ye wives, be in subjection to your own husbands; that, if any obey not the word, they also may without the word be won by the conversation of the wives;"*

The word subjection used in this verse is the Greek word, "**hypotássō** (hoop-ot-as'-so)." This verb means "to obey, to subject one's self, or to yield to one's admonition or advice." It is a Greek military term meaning "to arrange [troop divisions] in a military fashion under the command of a leader." In a non-military use, it was "a voluntary attitude of giving in or cooperating." Based on this definition we can see that an overbearing woman is unacceptable. She will never win her man over to God. And if he is already saved she is making her man miserable everyday. Stand up man of God and put the devil on the run as you bring your house and God's house back in order!

LAZARUS COME FORTH

John 11:43 *"And when he thus had spoken, he cried with a loud voice, Lazarus, come forth."*

The word Lazarus means "whom God helps." Men, we have been dead too long. We have been dead in helping our wives around the house, dead in helping our wives get the children off to school, and dead in helping our communities get better and the kingdom of God advance. We need to hear the loud voice of Jesus saying, "Come forth." The voice of Jesus needs to be heard over the voice of our flesh. His voice needs to be heard over the voice of foolish friends. He is the only one that can help men get out of their dead state.

The word "loud" used in John the eleventh chapter and verse forty three is the Greek word megas. It means "big, strong, mighty, virtue, power and authority." This Greek word speaks of things highly esteemed for its excellence. We need to speak with authority and call forth. We need men whose voice we highly esteem to call us out of our deadness.

The word "loud" speaks of the degree of intensity which Jesus used to get Lazarus up. He could have whispered but in this case God wanted us to know the emotions and affections used by Jesus to get his friend Lazarus out. Jesus was speaking mightily.

Today we must care enough to get our brother out. We must be willing to speak to our young boys or upcoming young men in our strong masculine tone given to us by God to strike fear in them. I remember the tone of Eddie Frank Sharpe (my natural father's voice). I remember the tone of Mr. Howard Stephen's voice (the neighbor next door who had four sons). I remember the tone of Coach Earl Miller my P.E. (Physical Education) teacher. I remember the tone of Coach Reginald Moss when we would play basketball in his back yard with his son Tony. I remember the tone of Apostle Michael Goings and his brother Pastor Earl Goings, awesome men of God who have spoken truth and revelations to my life. I remember the tone of Apostle Paul Thomas, a great man of God. My list could go on and on. None of these men speak or talk with any feminine traits at all. All of my father's brothers, Columbus (Pop), Joe, Arthur (Pee Wee), and Albert spoke with authority in my life. I had great respect for them all as men, even though they were far from perfect, yet they taught their children and family to respect authority. God in his grace and wisdom saw fit that I was raised around strong masculine men. Thank You Jesus!

Even today God in his grace has allowed me to be connected with strong toned men, like Apostle Mal Williams, Apostle Kenneth Anderson, Apostle Zebedee Shepard, Apostle Calvin Ellison, Apostle Tommy Ford, Apostle Norbert Simmons, Apostle Aaron McNair, Apostle Charles Lewis, Dr. Larry Carter, Bishop Jesse Blaylock, Bishop Wayne Sharpe, and many many others. There are way too many for me to name and count. I am so grateful that God did it and continues to bring me into contact with these types of Mega Men!

Many of us in the body of Christ have heard how important David "Pop" Winans, along with his son Marvin Winans, was in helping Pastor Donnie McClurkin in finding his way out of a lifestyle of negative behavior. Pop Winans tone was strong and enforcing. Notice Marvin, Carvin, Michael, and Bee Bee all have strong tones. Even the late, great Ronald Winans had a strong tone. Plus their lifestyle was instrumental in helping to bring Donnie into his purpose and destiny of writing and singing songs that have touched and blessed lives all around the world. They helped him come forth. Now it is your time!

WHAT AREAS ARE MEN COMING FORTH IN?

1. THE LIGHT OF YOUR RIGHTEOUSNESS

"Commit thy way unto the Lord; trust also in him; and he shall bring it to pass. And he shall bring forth thy righteousness as the light, and thy judgment as the noonday." (Psalms 37:5, 6 KJV)

"Open up before God, keep nothing back; he'll do whatever needs to be done: He'll validate your life in the clear light of day and stamp you with approval at high noon." (Psalm 37:5, 6 MSG)

2. YOUR HEALTH

"Then shall thy light break forth as the morning, and thine health shall spring forth speedily: and thy righteousness shall go before thee; the glory of the Lord shall be thy rereward." (Isaiah 58:8 KJV)

13

3. YOUR ASSIGNMENT AND THE CHURCH

"Then Mordecai commanded to answer Esther, Think not with thyself that thou shalt escape in the king's house, more than all the Jews. For if thou altogether holdest thy peace at this time, then shall there enlargement and deliverance arise to the Jews from another place; but thou and thy father's house shall be destroyed: and who knoweth whether thou art come to the kingdom for such a time as this?" (Est. 4:13, 14)

"And Jesus answered and said unto him, Blessed art thou, Simon Bar-jona: for flesh and blood hath not revealed it unto thee, but my Father which is in heaven. [18] And I say also unto thee, That thou art Peter, and upon this rock I will build my church; and the gates of hell shall not prevail against it. [19] And I will give unto thee the keys of the kingdom of heaven: and whatsoever thou shalt bind on earth shall be bound in heaven: and whatsoever thou shalt loose on earth shall be loosed in heaven." (Matt. 16:17-19)

4. YOUR FINANCES

"They prevented me in the day of my calamity: but the Lord was my stay. He brought me forth also into a large place; he delivered me, because he delighted in me." (Psalms 18:18, 19)

"He brought them forth also with silver and

gold: and there was not one feeble person among their tribes. And he brought forth his people with joy, and his chosen with gladness: And gave them the lands of the heathen: and they inherited the labour of the people;" (Psalms105:37, 43, 45)

I truly believe that God wants to help men get it together financially. We have to help other men make better financial choices. We must learn to use our buying power in a more productive way. We must learn to purchase those things that bring economic empowerment, like real estate and not just shoes and clothes. We must learn to save more and spend less so that we can be debt free and not leave our families in a lot of debt. We as men must stop trying to just look wealthy, but we must seek to make intelligent financial choices that will produce wealth for us and the next generation.

BE AGRESSIVE

One preacher said, "You have to work your mind and get off your behind." Aggressive means "making an all-out effort to win or succeed; vigorously energetic, especially in the use of initiative and forcefulness: boldly assertive, forward and pushy." In most sports today the player or team that is the most aggressive usually wins. It is not always the team with the most talent or the most gifted player or players, but rather the most aggressive team that ends up taking home the trophy.

The motto for the Oakland Raiders was "Just Win Baby." Yes their owner, Al Davis believed in just winning. Jack Tatum, Howie Long and others believed and lived by it. It was how they played, and it is what led the franchise to winning four Super Bowls thus far. In other words this owner was challenging his team to not make excuses but give all their energy and efforts to winning. He was telling them to be assertive. Those who saw the Oakland Raiders play during those successful years saw a team that was pushy. They had a defense that was intimidating. Receivers who caught a pass paid a high price as they ran across the middle or jumped up into the air.

I believe as men we should demonstrate this same

type of aggression as it relates to our lives. We should take the bull by the horn and forcefully take territory from the enemy. Winston Churchhill said, "History is going to be kind to me because I intend to write it." We must not be mired in the mud of mediocrity. We must aggressively make the pages of our story read the way we want the script to read. We have to forcefully move our lives in the direction that we want it to go.

> Mark 10:46-52 *"And they came to Jericho: and as he went out of Jericho with his disciples and a great number of people, blind Bartimaeus, the son of Timaeus, sat by the highway side begging. [47] And when he heard that it was Jesus of Nazareth, he began to cry out, and say, Jesus, thou Son of David, have mercy on me. [48] And many charged him that he should hold his peace: but he cried the more a great deal, Thou Son of David, have mercy on me. [49] And Jesus stood still, and commanded him to be called. And they call the blind man, saying unto him, Be of good comfort, rise; he calleth thee. [50] And he, casting away his garment, rose, and came to Jesus. [51] And Jesus answered and said unto him, What wilt thou that I should do unto thee? The blind man said unto him, Lord, that I might receive my sight. [52] And Jesus said unto him, Go thy way; thy faith hath made thee whole. And immediately he received his sight, and followed Jesus in the way."*

Notice the aggression in this blind man. In spite of being told by the disciples of Jesus "to be quiet," this man kept yelling out to Jesus. In fact he yelled louder when they told him to hold his peace. He refused to not get his request granted. He is called "son of Timaeus" which means unclean. Men need to cry out to God today because we are sons of unclean men. This goes all the way back to the first Adam or man who caused us to be defiled. It also applies to our present day fathers who haven't known Jesus Christ as Lord and Saviour. Their uncleanness has caused us to be blind and not be able to see our way in raising our children, loving our wives or finishing relationships that we start. Our fathers' uncleanness has caused us not to be able to have a vision for our lives, but thank God we can cry out and get our sight. We must aggressively cry out to Jesus for mercy. We must cry out to him and allow him to cleanse us from all unrighteousness through his blood. Even if other men tell us to leave Jesus alone, we must refuse to listen to them.

It was easy for the disciples to tell this man to be quiet because they could see what a barking dog, a house, or a synagogue look like. The blind man could not. Those who can see might not understand this type of aggression but those who are blind will. Moreover those who were once blind and can now see will understand why you are so aggressively pursuing Jesus.

This aggression is not based on pride, but is birthed through humility. It is based on our need for change and our desire to be better men. Bartimaeus didn't care what the disciples thought about him because he was after his deliverance. He was tired of being blind, and he was probably tired of begging. He was ready to lend a helping hand instead of being the one in need of a helping hand. I truly believe that some men who read this book are tired

18

of begging and are about to see a reversal take place. You are about to see and help other men rise to new levels. They will cast off their beggars garment and run to Jesus for healing.

> Acts 1:9-11 *"And when he had spoken these things, while they beheld, he was taken up; and a cloud received him out of their sight. [10] And while they looked stedfastly toward heaven as he went up, behold, two men stood by them in white apparel; [11] Which also said, Ye men of Galilee, why stand ye gazing up into heaven? this same Jesus, which is taken up from you into heaven, shall so come in like manner as ye have seen him go into heaven."*

Men have no time to stand around gazing. The disciples were in awe of Jesus, and they had every right to be amazed by a man going up in the clouds, but they failed to hear his words to go tarry until they were endued with power from on high. They didn't understand that he wanted them to go and do greater works than he had done. I know that when I am dead and gone, I want whoever takes over to do greater works than I did. Horace Mann said, "We should be ashamed to die until we have made some major contribution to human kind." Wow, this awesome statement requires every male to take the initiative of being a trailblazer. Henry David Roe said, "Do not go Where ever the path may lead, go where there is no path and leave a trail."

> Hebrews 6:12 *"That ye be not slothful, but followers of them who through faith and patience inherit the promises."*

"In order that you may not grow disinterested and become [spiritual] sluggards, but imitators, behaving as do those who through faith (by their leaning of the entire personality on God in Christ in absolute trust and confidence in His power, wisdom, and goodness) and by practice of patient endurance and waiting are [now] inheriting the promises." (Hebrews 6:12 AMP)

> *"Don't drag your feet. Be like those who stay the course with committed faith and then get everything promised to them."* (Hebrews 6:12 MSG)

We must not be slothful. You might say to me, "Bishop Van Sharpe I want to be aggressive." I will start by saying this to you that before you become an aggressive leader, you must be an aggressive follower.

1. AGGRESSIVE FOLLOWERS

It is imperative that you follow someone aggressively.
Some people claim to have followed some leaders aggressively and the truth of the matter is they never have or couldn't maintain it. They were never faithful to a Bible class or faithful in paying tithes. Yet they claim to have followed their pastor. Some show up once the pastor has called them or allowed a deacon or member to check on them. That is not what I'm talking about. The disciples of Jesus aggressively followed him. Elisha aggressively followed Elijah.

> 2 Kings 2:9-10 KJV
> *"And it came to pass, when they were gone over, that Elijah said unto Elisha, Ask what I shall do*

for thee, before I be taken away from thee. And Elisha said, I pray thee, let a double portion of thy spirit be upon me. [10] And he said, Thou hast asked a hard thing: nevertheless, if thou see me when I am taken from thee, it shall be so unto thee; but if not, it shall not be so."

2. AGGRESSIVE LEADERS

Remember those who aggressively follow become aggressive leaders. Jesus knew that he could raise up all twelve of his apostles to be aggressive leaders if they followed him that way. He knew that they would have to lead the way once he departed physically from the earth. Also, remember AGRESSIVE leaders give wise advice and they Finish the Deal.

> Proverbs 24:6 *"For by wise counsel thou shalt make thy war: and in multitude of counsellors there is safety."*

> Proverbs 20:18 *"Every purpose is established by counsel: and with good advice make war."*

SIX AREAS FOR MEN TO BE AGRESSIVE IN

1. AGRESSIVE IN LOVE

We need men that will walk in love like Jesus did!

2. AGRESSIVE IN PRAYER

We need men that will pray without ceasing and cover everything and everybody with prayer!

3. AGRESSIVE IN THE WORD

We need men that will meditate in the word day and night!

4. AGRESSIVE IN PRAISE

We need men that will praise God like a wild man with reckless abandon!

5. AGRESSSIVE GIVERS

We need men who refuse to rob God or be stingy!

6. AGRESSIVE TOWARD WINNING SOULS

We need men who aren't afraid or ashame to share their faith with other men and women!

BRINGING THINGS TO REST

Aggresive leaders and men bring their families, their communities, and their nation, governments, and the church into REST!

> Matthew 11:28-29
> *"Come unto me, all ye that labour and are heavy laden, and I will give you rest. [29] Take my yoke upon you, and learn of me; for I am meek and lowly in heart: and ye shall find rest unto your souls."*

Jesus as the perfect man in the earth was urging everybody to come to him so that he could bring them to rest. He is still inviting us into his rest today. In a day and time like this we should accept the invitation and experience this vital liberation. He wants to bring us out of a state of worry and confusion. These times don't have to defeat us or take us into fear and panic. Jesus provides rest for our souls.

> Chronicles 22:9-10 *"Behold, a son shall be born to thee, who shall be a man of rest; and*

I will give him rest from all his enemies round about: for his name shall be Solomon, and I will give peace and quietness unto Israel in his days. [10] He shall build an house for my name; and he shall be my son, and I will be his father; and I will establish the throne of his kingdom over Israel for ever."

Solomon as king of Israel was called and chosen by God to bring them into peace or rest. It was during his reign or rule that the nation wouldn't have to experience war. God wanted his people to be in peace and tranquility so he raised up Solomon to build a house for his name. **Solomon** means "peace." God wants his house and your home to be a place of peace. It shouldn't be a place where fighting and fussing goes on.

I remember as a little boy growing up I would hate to hear my mom and dad argue. It would be frightening because I would be afraid that he would hit my mom, or they would fight each other and someone would get killed. Thank God that none of those things ever happened, yet my heart would beat very fast and fear would grip me when I would hear my father raise his voice at my mom. I think every child has similar feelings as they hear their parents argue or yell at each other. I refuse to solve problems this way especially in front of children. This must be your resolve as a man.

Even in the house of God men are there to keep peace. You shouldn't do things that cause the visionary to lose sleep or lose hope. As a man you aren't there to cause confusion or wars but rather to function as elders and deacons to keep peace.

It is a sign of immaturity and a lack of understanding

if you believe fussing solves anything. Your people skills need help if you seek to solve disagreements with violence or anger. I had an elder who left the church that I pastor who said that I said I would slap him side his head. That was a total lie because when you've been pastoring 30 years you totally understand that violence is never God's way. He said that what I didn't recognize that he was carrying a gun and would have either shot me or beat me with the end of the gun. Think about how silly this sounds for a person in God's house to talk like this. Silly isn't it? Immature and foolish isn't it?

> *"Keep your temper under control; it is foolish to harbor a grudge."* (Ecclesiastes 7:9 GNT)

I wrote a book a few years ago called "Sheep Taming Wolves" that teaches nonviolence. It teaches meekness. When this elder left the church, he claimed that I was jealous of him and laughed at him to his face when he told me what God had told him he would do when nothing could be further from the truth. This is why when you counsel some people, you need witnesses in the room with you because people will lie to justify their rebellion or what they want to do. The only reason he was even approached was because of trying to seduce people out of the church like an Absalom. However, I never demonstrated any anger or resentment. In fact, that night when he left I hugged him. He went out and lied and said I told him that his marriage would break up and other terrible things. I wrote another book years ago called "Don't Lose Yours Trying To Save Theirs." Think about it when a family breaks up, what glory would any man of God get out of that? I guarantee if you ask anybody who was in that room they would tell you that I said no such thing. He also lied and said that I got on the phone and told other pastors not to have anything to do with him. This was yet another lie. I never did that or would do that. I never sent a letter out or called anyone about him. Even though in some cases doing that may be appropriate, yet I have never done it throughout all my years of pastoring.

On a previous occasion this man had lied to a lady who had come to our church. He had told this lady that he had attended Shaw University and had a degree from Shaw and had promised to help her get a job based on where he was working and what he was being paid. This lady was furious when she learned the truth. He had told the lady that he was a pastor and all kinds of lies. Time want even allow me to tell all of the lies. My wife and I met with him and his wife. The lady was furious about these lies because it almost caused her not to get her degree because she needed qualified signatures on certain papers to turn in to her professors. When this confrontation was made, he had to apologize to the lady. The lady looked at my wife and I, and I told her that I really did go to Shaw, and I really did have a degree in Mass Communication. Also I told her that my wife really did attend Shaw and she had a degree as well in Speech Pathology. Out of all this my wife and I still tried to help this elder. Yet he made a crazy statement about a gun on social media. Because of the pattern of lying that I saw, I knew it would be to the ministry's best interest to have several witnesses when counseling him about anything. And I am glad I did. it was never to set him up, but instead it was to avoid any dispute about what was said during counseling of any sort. Those who were present know the truth and so does God.

This is why you as a man must know that you are called to bring peace and not war to the house of God. Otherwise you will do things like carnal minded men who don't know the word of God. Our streets are filled with violence and people constantly die in our black communities because they don't know how to disagree without thinking violently. I have never counseled people in all my 30 years where I have behaved violently towards anyone. Every pastor knows that you aren't mad at people for leaving the church that you pastor. You want people to do and be better than you. Yet, when their motive is to destroy or blame you, then you are disappointed because of all that you have invested in them and helped them with, but you are never violent. I am amazed that a man that I had prayed for who was dying of prostrate cancer would think such foolishness. He was a man that I quoted scriptures to when he was talking about dying and leaving his family behind. Yet I encouraged him to live and not die. When this man's mother was in ICU in a hospital in Greenville and doctors had given up on her, God spoke to me and said, "This sickness was not unto death." I told him what I heard the Lord say when he called crying because he thought it was over for his mom. My wife and I went to the hospital standing on what God said. We walked in that hospital room where she was lying on that bed. The Lord told me before I got there not to consider her body or how it looked. We prayed for his mom and God brought her out of that situation. Glory to God! Yet he talked about physically hurting me. Men we have to do better than this. Bring things to rest not destruction!

Dr. Martin Luther King Jr. said,
"Tough-mindedness without
tenderheartedness is cold and detached,
leaving one's life in a perpetual winter devoid
of the warmth of spring and the gentle heat
of summer."

Every man must recognize that you are in the house, neighborhood and nation to bring everything to rest. As a man, the way God has wired you is that you have the ability like Noah to bring your family into the ark and guide them through turbulent times. You have the ability to withstand the storm without getting hysterical. You have been called to keep everything in your house calm. God created you so that you would be able to guide your house like Noah whose name means "rest" did. He kept everything in the ark until the waters were abated or brought to an end.

> Genesis 8:3-4 *"And the waters returned from off the earth continually: and after the end of the hundred and fifty days the waters were abated. [4] And the ark rested in the seventh month, on the seventeenth day of the month, upon the mountains of Ararat."*

I hope every man notices in the verses that the waters returned off the earth at the end of 150 days. This is the total of five months. I believe every man has the grace of God on them to lead their household through the floods of life until they come to an end. God's grace will outlast the things that have drowned those who refuse to rely on his grace. As a man you must not be too proud to ask

God to help you through the waters. NOTHING is better than having God on your side.

> Psalm 124:2-4 *"If it had not been the Lord who was on our side, when men rose up against us: [3] Then they had swallowed us up quick, when their wrath was kindled against us: [4] Then the waters had overwhelmed us, the stream had gone over our soul:"*

> 2 Timothy 4:16-17
> *"At my first answer no man stood with me, but all men forsook me: I pray God that it may not be laid to their charge. [17] Notwithstanding the Lord stood with me, and strengthened me; that by me the preaching might be fully known, and that all the Gentiles might hear: and I was delivered out of the mouth of the lion."*

It is also impotant to note that God allowed Noah to rest the ark in the seventh month. We know seven is the blessed and sanctified number. We as men have been given by God's grace to bring everything commmitted to our hands to a blessed and sanctified place. Hallelujah! The devil has tried to spew out venomous lies in hope that men would believe that they aren't necessary or needed. He wants you as a man to denounce your value. Satan wants you to relinquish your authority and surrender your might to him. In spite of how strong your wife and family may seem without you, they are stronger with you if you will accept the challenge and the responsibility of who God has called you to be. Notice, God didn't tell Noah's wife to build an ark; he told Noah. Neither did he tell her to gather the animals to go into the ark. He told Noah. He had the assignment over his life. Men we have this assignment. We can't be replaced by a female or a robot. We have the ball in our court. So let the game begin!

> Genesis 8:4 *"And the ark rested in the seventh month, on the seventeenth day of the month, upon the mountains of Ararat."*

Also notice that the ark rested upon the mountains of Ararat. The word **Ararat** in the Hebrew means "the cursed is reversed." We as men have the ability to take our families, communities, and nation to a mountain that reverses the curses that have plagued them. Spiritual men can reverse the curses that are in our land due to corrupt imaginations. We can reverse the curse of violence and take our families to a place of non-violence. We can reverse the curse of drugs and bring our families into sobriety. We can reverse the curse of poverty and bring our brothers and families into the fullness of their inheritance that belongs to them through the blood of Jesus, the cross and his resurrection!

BRING UP A GENERATION ON YOUR KNEES

> Genesis 50:19-23 *"And Joseph said unto them, Fear not: for am I in the place of God? [20] But as for you, ye thought evil against me; but God meant it unto good, to bring to pass, as it is this day, to save much people alive. [21] Now therefore fear ye not: I will nourish you, and your little ones. And he comforted them, and spake kindly unto them. [22] And Joseph dwelt in Egypt, he, and his father's house: and Joseph lived an hundred and ten years. [23] And Joseph saw Ephraim's children of the third generation: the children also of Machir the son of Manasseh were brought up upon Joseph's knees."*

Some of my fondest memories in my life have been playing with my daughter when she was little. I used to play patty cake and sing all kinds of songs to her as she sat on my knees. Today I play with my little grandson the same way. As they are on your knees, you get a chance to nourish them and impart things into them while they are having fun. I taught my little grandson how to pray as I had him on my knees. Today I laugh as this two year old child puts his hands together and closes his eyes and prays. Men we don't have to have perverted minds. We should be able to nourish our little daughters and sons up on our knees without molesting them. We as men should speak kind words and comforting words to our families as they sit on our knees and develop into vessels that will glorify God. Joseph knew he had been put in the place of God for his family.

> Proverbs 20:6-7 *"Most men will proclaim every one his own goodness: but a faithful man who can find? [7] The just man walketh in his integrity: his children are blessed after him."*

Notice Joseph saw three generations of children. He was able to share with them many of his life lessons. Unfortunately many men are learning by bumping their heads because they don't have their father's placing them on their knees and sharing life lessons with them. I truly believe generations have suffered because nobody put them on their knees. I love telling my little grandson things I have learned and watching his little eyes light up as he tries to comprehend what I am talking about. He loves hearing me sing the song "Awesome" as he tries to play the drums. I think it is time that men bring this powerful and meaningful element back to the home. I know it won't solve every problem but I think it will keep our younger generation in touch with the older generation and help to eliminate the generation gaps. It also creates a dynamic bond. I remember when my grandson was first born, he would barely come to me. He would go to my daughter and my wife. Today he will cry if I leave his presence. He wants to go with me everywhere. My daughter was the same way when she was little.

I admonish you to put that little child on your knees and talk to them, pray for them, hug them and kiss your grandchildren because they need it to develop into a loving person. Far too many of our young boys and girls during their childhood are being hit, kicked or punched instead of being prayed for, hugged, kissed and loved. It is time for men to change that!

SHOW THYSELF A MAN

1 Kings 2:1-3 *"Now the days of David drew nigh that he should die; and he charged Solomon his son, saying, [2] I go the way of all the earth: be thou strong therefore, and shew thyself a man; [3] And keep the charge of the Lord thy God, to walk in his ways, to keep his statutes, and his commandments, and his judgments, and his testimonies, as it is written in the law of Moses, that thou mayest prosper in all that thou doest, and whithersoever thou turnest thyself:"*

These potent verses written by King David to his son, Solomon must resonate in the heart of every man seeking to answer the call of manhood and seeking to leave a legacy behind for his family or other men. It is not a charge to be strong physically, but it is a charge to demonstrate inner strength. It is a charge to understand that things will require inner fortitude that comes from God and his word. The times we are living in are truly calling for us not to run, but demonstrate a courage that we make demons back up. It is easy to quit or run, especially when things get chaotic. Many men have gone physically and emotionally from the home, community and the church. Some have decided to check out through suicide. Yet we must encourage men to find strength from God and his word.

Statistics tell us that 84 percent of our homes are being run by women. This is because we didn't see a father, or we saw our daddy's run. Plus slavery taught black men to make a baby but not take care of them.

Slavery taught us to be a stud. Black men were called upon to create more babies to help white men have more slaves to work their farms. The stronger he was outwardly the more this process worked.

Today many of our black men are caught up in "Street Credibility." One out of every three males will go to jail before they are thirty. Over sixty-two percent will be incarcerated who drop out of school before they are thirty. Eighty percent of those who drop out disqualify themselves from public jobs. They can't get public housing, nor can they work for the federal government or become an attorney. They are eliminated from professional jobs which resign them to a life of crime or poverty. They call it street credibility when in reality all it truly is, is playing into the hands of the adversary.

Let me make it clear that if you are courageous; you can beat these odds. Plus, through courage you can come out of jail and become the next Judge Matthis. It has been said that, "Adversity introduces a man or a woman to themself." As one who understands that I am my brother's keeper, I want to encourage you to push pass the restrictions and limitations of your past and press into the potential of your future. In spite of your past record there is a job out there with your name on it. Be courageous enough to keep looking until you find it.

Every man must be courageous in the midst

of his generation and peers to live in line with the commandments of God. Even when you miss it, repent and get back up and do it God's way! Build with the materials that God has given you. HE HAS SUPPLIED ALL THAT YOU NEED! You must get around wise hearted men that are skilled to help you make the kind of garments that you can minister to God in!

> Exd 28:3 *And thou shalt speak unto all that are wise hearted, whom I have filled with the spirit of wisdom, that they may make Aaron's garments to consecrate him, that he may minister unto me in the priest's office.*

I AM MY BROTHER'S KEEPER

Genesis 4:8-12 *"And Cain talked with Abel his brother: and it came to pass, when they were in the field, that Cain rose up against Abel his brother, and slew him. [9] And the Lord said unto Cain, Where is Abel thy brother? And he said, I know not: Am I my brother's keeper? [10] And he said, What hast thou done? the voice of thy brother's blood crieth unto me from the ground. [11] And now art thou cursed from the earth, which hath opened her mouth to receive thy brother's blood from thy hand; [12] When thou tillest the ground, it shall not henceforth yield unto thee her strength; a fugitive and a vagabond shalt thou be in the earth."*

Genesis 4:9 *"And the Lord said unto Cain, Where is Abel thy brother? And he said, I know not: Am I my brother's keeper?"*

In order for men to make the impact in society and in the church we must have men around us who see themselves as their brother's keeper. The kingdom of God is based upon us helping each other reach our fullest potential in

God. God gave Abel the desire and the ability to work with sheep, but he gave Cain the desire and ability to be a tiller of the ground. Neither probably could have done each other's job. The good thing is that God never asked them to. He wanted to bless them in their giftings.

We recognize that Cain saw that God blessed the offering that Abel brought to God more than the one he gave. This angered Cain and caused him to murder his brother and bury him. Abel's blood cried out to God, and God asked Cain, where is Abel thy brother? Notice God doesn't just ask him where is Abel, but he said, "thy brother." Cain's response was "I don't know. Am I my brother's keeper?" The answer to that question needs to be a big "Yes" by every man in the kingdom of God. Yes you are your brother's keeper.

I believe since we who are men know exactly what it is like to be a man; we owe it to each other to assist each other on our journey. Jesus sent his disciples out two by two so that they could help establish the word and so that they could encourage each other as they faced demonic opposition. It is important that men help men reach their destiny.

I have been blessed to have a tremendous natural and spiritual brother in the kingdom of God by the name of Bishop Ronald Wayne Sharpe. He is an awesome man of God, and we have been there for each other during highs and what looked like lows in ministry. I celebrate his successes, and he celebrates mine. Anything that I can do to help him in any way I am willing to do it.

I also have what I call other brothers in Christ from other mothers, and I desire to see only great things happen to them and through them. It doesn't matter that they are a part of a different denomination or a different color. I want them to succeed. It doesn't even matter if they haven't been pastoring as long as I have or have more members in their local assembly than I have. They are my brothers!

The drive by shootings and gangs in our cities have young men killing each other and when asked by the police, "Where is your brother?," they answer like Cain, "I don't know. Am I My brother's keeper?." They fail to understand that they are their brothers' keepers. As I have been ask to speak at men's conferences in different cities and states, one thing that I have discovered is that we have more in common than we have different from one another. It is on the basis of these similarities that we can be a strength to one another. For example, most men don't truly enjoy going shopping with their wives. Mainly it is because a woman will stay in a store or in one area for a very long period of time.

When my wife and mom go shopping, they can stay looking in a store for lengthy periods of time. Yes they come out with some great deals, but when I go with them, my wife usually tells me to go look around. She knows that it will be a while. I can go look in the men section, the appliance section, the toy section, and movie section and when I return they (my wife and mom) are still in the same section. Many men can relate to what I just said.

Therefore, if you ask a man about certain legitimate trials, tests and temptations, he can relate to them as well. We must encourage other men and help them stay motivated. We must help our brothers achieve their dreams. In order to do this we must be willing to lay down our lives for one another.

John 15:12-13 *"This is my commandment, That ye love one another, as I have loved you. [13] Greater love hath no man than this, that a man lay down his life for his friends."*

FOUR THINGS TO HELP KEEP YOUR BROTHER

1. PRAY FOR HIM

> Luke 22:31-32 *"And the Lord said, Simon, Simon, behold, Satan hath desired to have you, that he may sift you as wheat: [32] But I have prayed for thee, that thy faith fail not: and when thou art converted, strengthen thy brethren."*

Jesus knew that the devil had a covert attack designed to pull Peter down to nothing. However, Jesus prayed for him. We must do the same for other men. Peter who became a powerful Apostle of the Jews was preserved through the intercession of Jesus. Satan wanted to take the good stuff out of him, but because Jesus prayed, he was converted and was able to strengthen the brethren.

> Romans 8:26-27 *"Likewise the Spirit also helpeth our infirmities: for we know not what we should pray for as we ought: but the Spirit*

itself maketh intercession for us with groanings which cannot be uttered. [27] And he that searcheth the hearts knoweth what is the mind of the Spirit, because he maketh intercession for the saints according to the will of God."

2. SPEAK OFTEN TO HIM

Malachi 3:16 *"Then they that feared the Lord spake often one to another: and the Lord hearkened, and heard it , and a book of remembrance was written before him for them that feared the Lord , and that thought upon his name."*

Men truly need encouragement. We must not allow our pride make us fail to admit it. It has been said that for every negative statement that we hear about ourselves, we need to hear something in the positive direction at least seventeen times to remove those negative words. That fact alone should tell men how important it is for us to speak positive words often one to another, especially the words of Jesus which are spirit and life. We as men must make it our business to speak words that will encourage other men in the Lord and speak them often. It must become a priority for us!

3. REFUSE TO BE JEALOUS OF YOUR BROTHER'S SACRIFICE

Hebrews 11:4 *"By faith Abel offered unto God a more excellent sacrifice than Cain, by which he obtained witness that he was righteous, God testifying of his gifts: and by it he being dead yet speaketh.*"

One of the things that people fail to understand when they see the way a man of God has been blessed is their sacrifice. I know the sacrifice that I have made has been tremendous. My wife and I have sacrificed all kinds of time, talent, and finances into the kingdom of God. Yet, when people see the blessings show up, they think it came without us paying any kind of price. Abel made a greater sacrifice than Cain. Cain instead of getting jealous of his brother should have just been willing to make a sacrifice.

4. STRIVE TO BE AN EXAMPLE TO HIM

1 Peter 2:21 "*For even hereunto were ye called: because Christ also suffered for us, leaving us an example, that ye should follow his steps:*"

1 Timothy 4:12 "*Let no man despise thy youth; but be thou an example of the believers, in word, in conversation, in charity, in spirit, in faith, in purity.*"

In other words we must strive to walk upright. This is an ongoing process. We need every man helping each other in order to become better or more Christlike. It won't happen over night, but we must help each other continue to strive. Keep setting new marks for yourself. One man said, "When the end comes for you, let it find you conquering a new mountain, not sliding down an old one!"

Joshua 14:11-12 "*As yet I am as strong this day as I was in the day that Moses sent me: as my strength was then, even so is my strength now, for war, both to go out, and to come in. [12] Now therefore give me this mountain, whereof the Lord spake in that day; for thou heardest in that day how the Anakims were there, and that the cities were great and fenced: if so be the Lord will be with me, then I shall be able to drive them out, as the Lord said.*"

MIGHTY MEN OF VALOR

Joshua 1:13-15 *"Remember the word which Moses the servant of the Lord commanded you, saying, The Lord your God hath given you rest, and hath given you this land. [14] Your wives, your little ones, and your cattle, shall remain in the land which Moses gave you on this side Jordan; but ye shall pass before your brethren armed, all the mighty men of valour, and help them; [15] Until the Lord have given your brethren rest, as he hath given you, and they also have possessed the land which the Lord your God giveth them: then ye shall return unto the land of your possession, and enjoy it, which Moses the Lord's servant gave you on this side Jordan toward the sunrise."*

If there has ever been a time to be an armed mighty man, it is now, but even if you are not, this is still the time to find your help from a mighty man of valor. Joshua, as the leader of the nation of Israel, admonishes the mighty men to pass before their brethren and help them. Only the mighty men can help you get what your Heavenly Father has ordained. It is imperative that the mighty men of valor arise. Question: Do you see yourself as a mighty man who is armed and dangerous to the devil? Then God is telling you to help other brothers be what you are. If you have spiritual depth, how can you be satisfied until other brethren get some spiritual depth? If you have gotten your inheritance, how can you be satisfied knowing that there are other men or brethren around you still living in lack and being mommas' boys at age 30 and older? We have been given the call and the responsibility to cut off the head of every giant so that our brethren can Arise, Shout, Pursue, and Spoil the adversary. This is exactly what Judah did once they saw David cut off the head of Goliath.

> 1 Samuel 17:51-53 *"Therefore David ran, and stood upon the Philistine, and took his sword, and drew it out of the sheath thereof, and slew him, and cut off his head therewith. And when the Philistines saw their champion was dead, they fled. [52] And the men of Israel and of Judah arose, and shouted, and pursued the Philistines, until thou come to the valley, and to the gates of Ekron. And the wounded of the Philistines fell down by the way to Shaaraim, even unto Gath, and unto Ekron. [53] And the children of Israel returned from chasing after the Philistines, and they spoiled their tents."*

Mighty men of valor recognize that our champion, Jesus Christ, has defeated the devil; therefore, we can put the enemy to flight. As men see us being strong in The Lord and in the power of his might, they can gird themselves for battle. I love the definition of the word valour or valor. It means "boldness or determination in facing great danger, especially in battle." It means "heroic courage and bravery."

I believe that many men are being raised up by God for this time that will do heroic deeds in the nation and in the kingdom of God. These deeds of courage will be noteworthy because they will be right in the heat of battle. Many brethren will be rescued from the clutches of hell as these courageous acts are done. God is calling out to men everywhere to take courage and fight for our brethren. Our boldness will cause others to be bold. Our determination will authenticate that God chose the right men when he chose us and delivered us from the hand of the enemy. I believe as we pass before our brethren armed, we will receive our Medal of Honor. Many of us are running back into the war zone and retrieving our fallen brethren. The bullets, guns, and grenades are going off and being fired everywhere, yet we aren't afraid or timid. We have the whole armor of God on to take the spoil for our families and nation. Notice the women and children remain out of harm's way, but the men were called to be armed and fight. The Apostle Paul admonishes us in God's word to be strong,

> Ephesians 6:10 *"Finally, my brethren, be strong in the Lord, and in the power of his might."*

We need every man strapped and ready! It is not natural warfare, but spiritual warfare. Our brothers need help, and we must be like Forest Gump. In the midst of all the shooting and bombing, he ran back into the midst of the battle and rescued several of his fellow soldiers, including his captain. He knew they needed his help and even though he could run fast enough to escape, he decided to use his speed to bring out as many as he could. I believe that many of us are running back into the battle and assisting our fellow soldiers instead of being comfortable. My admonishment to you as a Man of God is "RUN FORREST RUN."

CONCLUSION
YOU DA MAN

Finally, I wish to exhort you as men through a poem written to me by my daughter when she was eighteen years old. It was written and read by her at my birthday celebration a few years ago. I believe with Jesus and the help of the Holy Spirit, we as men will rise up, take our place, and show our families, nation, and communities that we are "Da Man."

YOU DA MAN

Every since my life began
I realized that you da man
I saw your wisdom and courage too
and I learned I could rely on you.
Throughout my eighteen years you've worked
To provide me a happy life.
You've been there to help and give advice
And you did it all without strife
Your tolerant nature was really great

Nevertheless you'd not hesitate
To let me know when I'd been bad
It must have been hard, but that's being a dad
You're strong, smart, and filled with love
A gift to me from up above
So here's a greeting from your biggest fan
Happy Birthday Dad, cause You Da Man!

CPSIA information can be obtained at www.ICGtesting.com
Printed in the USA
BVOW07s0745221014

371713BV00001B/1/P